HOW TO HEAR
GOD'S VOICE:
Intro to the
Seer Gift-Understanding
Visions

BY
DEBORAH SANDOW

ISBN 978-1-60920-146-3
Printed in the United States of America

Library of Congress-in-Publication Data

API
Ajoyin Publishing, Inc.
P.O. Box 342
Three Rivers, MI 49093
www.ajoyin.com

Please direct your inquiries to admin@ajoyin.com

TABLE OF CONTENTS

INTRODUCTION

YOU MAY BE ASKING, "How do hearing and seeing relate to each other?" Have you ever heard the phrase "A picture is worth a thousand words"? Pictures are another way God may speak to us. Those pictures are what are often referred to in the Scriptures as visions. Can anyone have visions? That's what we are going to look into. What is a Seer? Simply enough, a Seer is one who sees in the Spirit.

Have you ever seen a motion out of the corner of your eye but when you looked, nothing was there? What did you do? Did you wonder what it was, or did you pooh-pooh it? I'd like to suggest that the motion was the beginning of seeing in the Spirit. This is God calling you to Him. Will you give God your attention when strange things happen or will you dismiss it?

Are you curious yet? I know I'm excited to share what I've learned over the years and how seeing in the Spirit has drawn me closer to God. In this Bible study we are going to look at what a Seer is and compare it to the gift of prophecy. We will discuss the purposes of the Seer gift. We are going to look at many different Seers in the Bible. We will look at the gift and who can have it. We will discuss the Spiritual World and ask: Is there one? In addition, we will practice ways to improve our ability to receive from God.

A.W. Tozer wrote:

Our pursuit of God is successful just because He is forever seeking to manifest Himself to us. The revelation of God to any man is not God coming from a distance upon a time to pay a brief and momentous visit to the man's soul. Thus, to think of it is to misunderstand it all. The approach of God to the soul or of the soul to God is not to be thought of in spatial terms at all. There is no idea of physical distance involved in the concept. It is not a matter of miles but of experience.

To speak of being near to or far from God is to use language in a sense always understood when applied to our ordinary human relationships. A man may say, "I feel that my son is coming nearer to me as he gets older," and yet that son has lived by his father's side since he was born and has never been away from home more than a day or so in his entire life. What then can the father mean? Obviously, he is speaking of experience. He means that the boy is coming to know him more intimately and with deeper understanding, that the barriers of thought and feeling between the two are disappearing, that father and son are becoming more closely united in mind and heart.

So, when we sing, "Draw me nearer, nearer, blessed LORD," we are not thinking of the nearness of place, but of the nearness of relationship. It is for increasing degrees of awareness that we pray, for a more perfect consciousness of the divine Presence. We need never shout across the spaces to an absent God. He is nearer than our own soul, closer than our most secret thoughts.

Why do some persons "find" God in a way that others do not? Why does God manifest His Presence to some and let multitudes of others struggle along in the half-light of imperfect Christian experience? Of course, the will of God is the same for all. He has no favorites within His household. All He has ever done for any of His children He will do for all of His children. The difference lies not with God but with us.

Pick at random a score of great saints whose lives and testimonies are widely known. Let them be Bible characters or well-known Christians of post-biblical times. You will be struck instantly with the fact that the saints were not alike. Sometimes the unlikenesses were so great as to be positively glaring. How different for example was Moses from Isaiah; how different was Elijah from David; how unlike each other were John and Paul, St. Francis and Luther, Finney and Thomas a' Kempis. The differences are as wide as human life itself- difference of race, nationality, education, temperament, habit and personal qualities. Yet they all walked, each in his day upon a high road of spiritual living far above the common way.

Their differences must have been incidental and in the eyes of God of no significance. In some vital quality they must have been alike. What was it?

I venture to suggest that the one vital quality which they had in commons was spiritual receptivity. Something in them was open to heaven, something which urged them Godward. Without attempting anything like a profound analysis, I shall say simply that they had spiritual awareness and that they went on to cultivate it until it became the biggest thing in their lives. They differed from the average person in that when they felt the inward longing, they did something about it. They acquired the lifelong habit of spiritual response. They were not disobedient to the heavenly vision. As David put it neatly, "when thou saidst, 'Seek ye my face'; my heart said unto thee, 'Thy face, LORD, will I seek.'"

As with everything good in human life, back of this receptivity is God. The sovereignty of God is here, and is felt even by those who have not placed particular stress upon it theologically. The pious Michael Angelo confessed this in a sonnet:

> *My unassisted heart is barren clay,*
> *That of its native self can nothing feed:*
> *Of good and pious works Thou art the seed,*
> *That quickens only where Thou sayest it may:*
> *Unless Thou show to us Thine own true way*
> *No Man can find it: Father! Thou must lead.*

These words will repay study as the deep and serious testimony of a great Christian.

Important as it is that we recognize God working in us, I would yet warn against a too great preoccupation with the thought. It is a sure road to sterile passivity. God will not hold us responsible to understand the mysteries of election, predestination and the divine sovereignty. The best and safest way to deal with these truths is to raise our eyes to God and in deepest reverence say, "O Lord, Thou knowest." Those things belong to the deep and mysterious Profound of God's omniscience. Prying into them may make theologians, but it will never make saints.

Receptivity is not a single thing; it is a compound of rather, a blending of several elements within the soul. It is an affinity for, a bent toward, a sympathetic response to, a desire to have. From this it may be gathered that it can be present in degrees, that we may have little or more or less, depending upon the individual. It may be increased by exercise or destroyed by neglect. It is not a sovereign and irresistible force which comes upon us as a seizure from above. It is a gift from God, indeed, but one which must be recognized and cultivated as any other gift if it is to realize the purpose for which it was given.[1]

The goal of this Bible study is to increase receptivity!

CHAPTER ONE
SPIRITUAL WORLD

I WANT TO FIRST EXPLAIN some of the language I'll use in this Bible study. In the Old Testament, a Seer was referred to as a man of God who'd, see in the Spirit. In this study, we'll look at Seers including Asaph, Jeremiah and Ezekiel to name a few.

In the New Testament, the word "Seer" is not used. Rather, the phrase   -vision- is used. In addition, there is a promise given in Acts 2 that all can see visions. In other words, everyone can see in the Spirit.

"And it shall come to pass in the last days, saith God, I will pour out of my Spirit upon all flesh: and your sons and your daughters shall prophesy, and your young men shall see visions, and your old men shall dream dreams" (Acts 2:17).

So, then, the concept of seeing in the Spirit is both an Old Testament and a New Testament way in which God speaks to His people.

In this chapter, I want to introduce you to the Spirit realm or Spiritual World. If a Seer is one who sees in the Spirit, what is the Spirit World? God is a three-part God, a -Triune God-. He consists of Father, Son and Holy Spirit. We also are three-part human being—body, soul and spirit. Both have a spirit, leading us to believe there is a spirit realm. The Bible tells us that battles are not fought with the flesh and blood (in the physical realm) but with powers and principalities (in the spirit realm). Thus, we may conclude that there is a good and a bad element to the spirit realm. This is the reason 1 John tells us not to trust every spirit. The Bible also tells us that things of the Spirit cannot be understood by the flesh, but are given by the Spirit and received by the Spirit. We cannot understand spiritual things with our minds (souls), but we must use our consciousnesses (spirits). The spirit of a man knows the deepest thoughts and motives. It's the deepest part of us.

Okay, I just threw a lot at you. Let's look at some Scriptures.

First, God is a triune God: Father, Son and Holy Spirit. Here is a Scripture referring to all three parts.

> *Go therefore and make disciples of all the nations, baptizing them in the name of the Father and of the Son and of the Holy Spirit, (Matt. 28:19).*

Second, we are three part human beings.

> *Now may the God of peace Himself sanctify you completely; and may your whole spirit, soul, and body be preserved blameless at the coming of our LORD Jesus Christ (1Thes. 5:23).*

*Circle the phrases **you completely** and **your whole.** What completes you? You are a complete being consisting of spirit, soul, and body.

Third, we can conclude that there is a physical world-- the world we can touch. In addition, there is a spiritual world which we cannot touch.

Fourth, our battles are not with the physical realm but with spiritual realm.

> *For we do not wrestle against flesh and blood, but against principalities, against powers, against the rulers of the darkness of this age, against spiritual hosts of wickedness in the heavenly places (Eph. 6:12).*

With this Scripture, we can conclude that there is a spiritual realm and learn how to fight in this spiritual realm. However, to fight, we must understand and see in the spiritual realm. In another Bible study in which I wrote, *"Why do bad things happen?"* there is a thorough teaching on Spiritual Warfare. This Bible study's goal, however, is to teach you how to see in the Spirit.

To have a battle, there must be two sides. Those sides are God's side and the enemy's side. How do we know which one we are seeing?

> *Beloved, do not believe every spirit, but test the spirits, whether they are of God; because many false prophets have gone out into the world (1John 4:1).*

In *"How to Hear God's Voice: Intro to Prophecy"*, I wrote a thorough teaching on testing the spirits. As a quick overview, whenever I see something in the Spirit, I pray and ask God if this is from Him. If it is not from God, I then tell what I see, "You need to leave, in Jesus' name". Angels are given an order from God and cannot go against that assignment. The being will not leave if it is from God. If it stays, I believe it is from God. I proceed by asking God what

He wants to tell me or show me. God has my total attention and I thank Him for speaking to me. Thus, the conversation continues. I will give you many examples of testing the Spirit throughout this study.

Fifth: your Spirit-man comes alive when you begin your relationship with Jesus Christ.

Because you have picked up this Bible study, you are probably curious about what the Bible is all about. Why else would you study it? If you have read the Old Testament, you have learned about a God who loves the people He created and He is always pursuing a relationship with them. He is a loving God who wants to bless and protect His people. However, He is also a jealous God, who wants to be worshipped as the one true God (see Exod. 20:5). He has set up laws for behavior, laws of nature, and spiritual laws. No matter whether you believe in God or not, these laws are upheld. If you plant a seed, you will reap that plant-- the Law of Nature. If you murder someone, you will be held accountable –the Laws of Behavior, better known as the Ten Commandments. If you seek God, you will find Him—the Spiritual Laws. One of the Spiritual Laws is that God will not and cannot allow sin or evil to be near Him. Unfortunately, all men are sinners (see Rom. 3:23). Whether it is in thought, word, or deed, all men have sinned.

So how does one get close to God? That's where the New Testament comes in. The first four books of the New Testament are called the Gospels. These books are about the life and death of Jesus Christ, the Son of Man. He came to earth, God in an incarnate body (see John 3:13). He came to teach more about Father God and how He loves mankind. He also came to pay the price for the sins of mankind (see John 3:16). Because of His willingness to pay mankind's debt, He makes Himself available to all. All you have to do is simply admit you are a sinner and ask Jesus to come into your heart and pay for your sins. He gladly does this. In addition, when you do this you are given another gift. That gift is the Holy Spirit (see 1 John 4:13). He comes into your consciousness and awakens your spirit. Now your spirit can receive from the Holy Spirit. This is often referred to as -being born again-, -asking Jesus into your heart-, -giving your life to Jesus- or -being saved-. Upon doing this, you become a child of God, your sins are forgiven, Jesus is your Savior, and you have the Holy Spirit within you. This opens up a world of adventure as you learn your new identity and authority. Watch for more Bible studies on these topics!

Final point: we cannot understand spiritual things with our minds. We are created with a spirit (wisdom, conscience, and communion) and a soul (mind, will and emotions). Spiritual things are understood only with our spirit.

> [10] *But God has revealed them to us through His Spirit. For the Spirit searches all things, yes, the deep things of God.* [11] *For what man knows the things of a man except the spirit of*

the man which is in him? Even so no one knows the things of God except the Spirit of God.
[12] Now we have received, not the spirit of the world, but the Spirit who is from God, that we might know the things that have been freely given to us by God.
[13] These things we also speak, not in words which man's wisdom teaches but which the Holy Spirit teaches, comparing spiritual things with spiritual. [14] But the natural man does not receive the things of the Spirit of God, for they are foolishness to him; nor can he know them, because they are spiritually discerned. [15] But he who is spiritual judges all things, yet he himself is rightly judged by no one. [16] For "who has known the mind of the LORD that he may instruct Him?" But we have the mind of Christ," (1Cor. 2:10-16).

*Underline the first sentence. Write it out.

*In your own words, write what this means.

*Circle all the capitalized **Spirit.**

*Write in your own words what this section of the Scriptures is saying.

*What are your thoughts? What are your questions? Which of these are new concepts to you?

If you have Jesus in your heart, you are also given the Sprit of God. The Spirit of God knows the deep things of God and He is willing to share, to teach and to reveal those things to you. The Spirit of God knows all things and is willing to   -freely give- you the understanding of all things.

Lord, there are Seers throughout the Scriptures, those who saw in the Spirit. Lord, teach me to see in the Spirit. Teach me the reasons and purposes of seeing in the Spirit. Prepare my heart for this gift of -Seeing in the Spirit- my character and my understanding. Stretch and grow my faith to receive from You in this new way. In Jesus' name; AMEN!

Let's recap:
1. God is a triune God.
2. You are a three-part being.
3. There is a physical realm and a spiritual realm.
4. Your battles are in the spiritual realm.
5. Your Spirit-man comes alive when you are born again of the Spirit.
6. The Holy Spirit reveals things to you through your spirit.

Journal Week One

Day 1

In this lesson the discussion was about a spiritual realm and the possibilities of seeing into it. You can see the raging battle. Here is an example in 2 Kings. The King of Syria wanted to attack Israel; however, his plans were continually spoiled. He thought he had a spy in his room. That wasn't the case. God was revealing to his prophet Elisha what was going on. Therefore, Elisha knew how to prepare for the fight. Elisha's servant didn't see in the spirit and was very afraid of what he saw in the physical realm.

> *Now the king of Syria was making war against Israel; and he consulted with his servants, saying, "My camp will be in such and such a place." ⁹ And the man of God sent to the king of Israel, saying, "Beware that you do not pass this place, for the Syrians are coming down there." ¹⁰ Then the king of Israel sent someone to the place of which the man of God had told him. Thus he warned him, and he was watchful there, not just once or twice.*
>
> *¹¹ Therefore the heart of the king of Syria was greatly troubled by this thing; and he called his servants and said to them, "Will you not show me which of us is for the king of Israel?"*
>
> *¹² And one of his servants said, "None, my Lord, O king; but Elisha, the prophet who is in Israel, tells the king of Israel the words that you speak in your bedroom."*
>
> *¹³ So he said, "Go and see where he is, that I may send and get him."*
>
> *And it was told him, saying, "Surely he is in Dothan."*
>
> *¹⁴ Therefore he sent horses and chariots and a great army there, and they came by night and surrounded the city. ¹⁵ And when the servant of the man of God arose early and went out, there was an army, surrounding the city with horses and chariots. And his servant said to him, "Alas, my master! What shall we do?"*
>
> *¹⁶ So he answered, "Do not fear, for those who are with us are more than those who are with them." ¹⁷ And Elisha prayed, and said, "Lord, I pray, open his eyes that he may see." Then the Lord opened the eyes of the young man, and he saw. And behold, the mountain was full of horses and chariots of fire all around Elisha. ¹⁸ So when the Syrians came down to him, Elisha prayed to the Lord, and said, "Strike this people, I pray, with blindness." And He struck them with blindness according to the word of Elisha. (2Kings 6:8-18).*

*Underline the phrase in verse 16 **Do not fear**.

This is very important to God. I have heard it said that there are 365 verses about fear. God does not want you to fear and He wants to remind you of this every day of the year. Fear puts up barriers to your communication with God and to your faith. Fear blocks God. Faith opens the door for God.

*What was Elisha's servant focusing on?

*What was Elisha focusing on?

Elisha was spending time with God. He knew what the enemy was doing without being near the enemy.

*Underline Elisha's prayer for his servant in verse 17. Write down what that prayer is.

Very interesting: One can pray to see in the spirit. His servant was not a prophet. *Can anyone see in the spirit?

For there is no partiality with God (Rom. 2:11).

The King James Version puts it this way

For there is no respect of persons with God (Rom.2:11 KJV).

Yes! All can see in the Spirit. Thank you Lord.

*Write down your hesitations or fears.

Many times throughout His ministry Jesus asks people to come. Come all who are weary. Come up here. Don't let your fears or misunderstandings stop you. Give them to God.

*Spend time writing out your prayers to Jesus.

Day 2

*Write about what you found to be a new concept in this lesson.

*Write down the questions that arose from this lesson.

Did you know God is watching you? God sees everything. He cares so much for you.

*Look up and write out these verses.

Job 36:7 (Remember you are righteous because of Jesus. You can include yourself in the group of the righteous.)

2Chronicles 16:9

Psalms 33:18

Psalm 32:8

Psalm 34:15

*What did you learn from these Scriptures?

*How do these Scriptures make you feel?

*Did it bring any images into your mind? Write about it.

*Did these Scriptures answer your questions or quiet your fears? Write about it.

Day 3

You are created in God's image (Gen. 1:26). If God actively watches you, do you think God wants you to actively watch? *Write down your thoughts.

Let's look at some Scriptures.

> *The LORD looked down from heaven upon the children of men, to see if there were any that did understand, and seek God(Psalm 14:2.KJV)*

*Who is actively watching?

> *My voice shalt thou hear in the morning, O LORD; in the morning will I direct my prayer unto thee, and will look up (Psalm 5:3.KJV)*

*Who is actively watching?

> *Then Jesus answered and said to them, "Most assuredly, I say to you, the Son can do nothing of Himself, but what He sees the Father do; for whatever He does, the Son also does in like manner(John 5:19).*

*Who is actively watching?

> *Watch and pray, lest you enter into temptation. The spirit indeed is willing, but the flesh is weak."(Matt. 26:41).*

*What does Jesus instruct you to do? Thought: If Jesus asked you (all) to watch, does that mean you (all) can see?

*What is a purpose of watching or the Seer gift?

*What do you think a person needs to do to prepare to watch or see?

We will discuss these last two questions in greater detail throughout this Bible study

Day 4

We have discussed many topics: the Spiritual Realm and that God reveals things to us through the Holy Spirit to our spirit. We have discussed that there are both good and evil in the Spiritual Realm. The best way to test the spirits is to test it against the Word of God. Does it say and act in a way that is in accordance with the Bible. Does it line up with the Word of God?

Let's practice seeing. Read through the following Scripture Psalm 23.

*As you are reading, are there **any phrases** that stick out to you.

*Are there any phrases that give you a **picture in your head**?

Just like when you are learning a language, you show a toddler an apple and say apple. Eventually, you can just say the word and the toddler knows what you're referring to.

*As you are reading this Scripture, what pictures do you see? Be sure to take note of those pictures.

> *The LORD is my shepherd;*
> *I shall not want.*
> *He makes me to lie down in green pastures;*
> *He leads me beside the still waters.*
> *He restores my soul;*
> *He leads me in the paths of righteousness*
> *For His name's sake.*
> *Yea, though I walk through the valley of the shadow of death,*
> *I will fear no evil;*

For You are with me;
Your rod and Your staff, they comfort me.
You prepare a table before me in the presence of my enemies;
You anoint my head with oil;
My cup runs over.
Surely goodness and mercy shall follow me
All the days of my life;
And I will dwell in the house of the LORD
Forever. (Psalm 23)

*What pictures did you see?

Hopefully you saw a shepherd and possibly some sheep. Take some time and let your imaginations go. Whoa. I just heard some of you put on the brakes. The word imagination may have put up some red flags. Let's look at some Scriptures.

From their callous hearts comes iniquity;
*their evil **imagination**s have no limits. (Psalm 73:7NIV).*

All day long I have held out my hands to an obstinate people,
*who walk in ways not good, pursuing their own **imagination**s—(Isaiah 65:2NIV).*

"Son of man, prophesy against the prophets of Israel who are now prophesying. Say to
*those who prophesy out of their own **imagination**:*
'Hear the word of the LORD!(Ezekiel 13:2NIV).

"Now, son of man, set your face against the daughters of your people who
*prophesy out of their own **imagination**. Prophesy against them (Ezekiel 13:17NIV).*

These verses give imagination a pretty bad reputation. But upon closer observation, what is imagination always associated with? Evil plans! Personal motivations!

Let's look at one more verse:

*Casting down **imagination**s and every high thing that exalts itself against the knowledge*
of God, bringing every thought into captivity to the obedience of Christ, (2 Cor. 10:5MEV).

Here the verse talks about casting down the imaginations that are against God. It doesn't mean that if your imagination is towards God or about a good thing that your imagination is bad. Think about how inventors invent. They think. They imagine. They experiment. They allow their brains to be stretched. They ask themselves questions: What about this? Why that? Why not this? If you're using your imagination to glorify God, to think about God, to allow your mind to stretch toward His infinite ways, imagination is not a bad thing. What are you like, O God? What are Your thought towards me? What would You have me do?

With that in mind, read the above Scripture again. Pray something like: Lord, open my eyes to see You as the Good Shepherd. Now, by faith, imagine what Jesus the Good Shepherd looks like. What are His facial expressions? What does He have in His hand? What do you feel- warmth, love or something else? Give yourself time to do this; three minutes or even 15 minutes. Set a timer and allow yourself the freedom to see.

*Use this space to write about what you saw. This is all Scriptural; you are setting your mind upon Jesus. Allow Him to show you how He feels about you.

Day 5

Let me pray over you like Elisha prayed for his servant: "Lord, I pray, open the reader's eyes that he/she may see." By faith, begin to thank God for what He wants to show or reveal to you. As you read this section of Revelation 19, be open to what God may show you.

Now I saw heaven opened, and behold, a white horse. And He who sat on him was called Faithful and True, and in righteousness He judges and makes war. His eyes were like a flame of fire, and on His head were many crowns. He had a name written that no one knew except Himself. He was clothed with a robe dipped in blood, and His name is called The Word of God. And the armies in heaven, clothed in fine linen, white and clean, followed Him on white horses. Now out of His mouth goes a sharp sword, that with it He should strike the nations. And He Himself will rule them with a rod of iron. He Himself treads the winepress of the fierceness and wrath of Almighty God. And He has on His robe and on His thigh a name written:

KING OF KINGS AND
LORD OF LORDS (Rev.19:11-16).

*What did you see?

*What did you emotionally feel?

*What did you physically feel?

*Did you hear any sounds associated with the picture you saw?

*Use this space to write about this experience.

*Read Revelations again and allow yourself more time to ponder the picture you have in your mind.

*Underline words that bring images to your mind. Can you add more detail to what you wrote above? God is infinite and He always has more to share- IF you will take the time.

* Use this space to write your thoughts.

*Read these Scriptures.

<u>Exodus 14:14</u>
The Lord will fight for you, and you shall hold your peace.

<u>Exodus 14:25</u> And He took off their chariot wheels, so that they drove them with difficulty; and the Egyptians said, "Let us flee from the face of Israel, for the Lord fights for them against the Egyptians."

<u>Exodus 15:3</u> The Lord *is* a man of war; The Lord *is* His name.

<u>Deuteronomy 1:30</u> The Lord your God, who goes before you, He will fight for you, according to all He did for you in Egypt before your eyes,

<u>Deuteronomy 3:22</u> You must not fear them, for the Lord your God Himself fights for you.

<u>Deuteronomy 20:4</u> For the Lord your God *is* He who goes with you, to fight for you against your enemies, to save you.'

<u>Joshua 23:10</u> One man of you shall chase a thousand, for the Lord your God *is* He who fights for you, as He promised you.

*How do these Scriptures match with the picture you were given from Revelation 19?

*Circle examples in each Scripture. Write your thoughts here.

*Can you add to your description of Jesus as the Commander-in-Chief of the Armies of Heaven? Write down your ideas in this space.

CHAPTER TWO
WHAT IS A SEER?
HOW DO I BECOME ONE?

IN THE STRONG'S EXHAUSTIVE Concordance, I found there are many Hebrew words for **seer**. The most common definition is: **a seer is a person who has visions, one who looks and prophesies**. Some of the other definitions were **timely** (5718), **keeper of records** (2335), **gatherer** (623), **leader of choir of the temple**(3038), **to establish, found, or fix**(883) and **gatekeeper** (7778).

Now that we know what a Seer is, how do we become one?

The first step is to ask. We have discussed the example of where Elisha asked God to open the eyes of his servant to see.

> *If you then, being evil, know how to give good gifts to your children, how much more will your Father who is in heaven give good things to those who ask Him! (Matt. 7:11)*

Jesus is saying that God the Father has good gifts for you. All you must do is ask. Think about this: when you became saved you asked God for salvation. You believed that God wanted to save you and that you were saved. It took a step of faith. It is the same with the Seer Gift. He is a good father with good gifts to give you. That's the closeness of the relationship that God wants with you. God wants to develop a deeper relationship with you. He wants to reveal Himself to you. Just ask!

Dear Heavenly Father, open my eyes that I may know You more. Open my eyes of understanding and revelation that I may grow closer to You. In Jesus' name I pray, AMEN

The second step is to worship.

There is a man in the Bible named Asaph(interestingly enough, his name means **gatherer** which is one of the definitions of Seer). He was a seer. He did not, however, start out with the title of a seer.

He was the son of Berechiah, and was a Levite from the Gershom family. In 1 Chronicles 15 King David appointed captains of groups of the Levites. He then asked the captains to appoint their brothers as singers to sing joyful songs. They were also to appoint from those singers people to play the lyre, harp, and cymbals. Asaph was among those appointed and he was to play the cymbals. (See 1 Chronicles 15:11-16)

In 1 Chronicles 16 David appointed Levites to minister before the Ark of the LORD, to make petitions and to give thanks and praise to God. Among those appointed was Asaph, who was made chief of this group. He continued to play the cymbals. Notice here, the king appointed Asaph- a real promotion! (See 1 Chronicle 16:4-6)

On that day, David personally handed a psalm of thanksgiving to the LORD he had written to Asaph. Asaph had the attention of the king. Asaph was trusted by the king to lead (See 1 Chronicle 16:7-36)

Later, in 1 Chronicles 25, David appointed some of Asaph's sons to prophecy, sing, and play. Not only had Asaph prophesied under the king's supervision, but Asaph had taught his sons to prophecy and play praises to God. (See 1 Chronicles 25:1-5)

Moreover King Hezekiah and the leaders commanded the Levites to sing praise to the LORD with the words of David and of Asaph the seer. So they sang praises with gladness, and they bowed their heads and worshiped. (2 Chron. 29:30).

Asaph was also given the title of **Seer** and the psalms he wrote were remembered and played. He is given credit for writing Psalms 50, 73, 76, 77, 81, 82, and 83

From Asaph, we learn that God is looking for worshippers. He was promoted, so we can conclude he did a good job. He was **trustworthy**, so much so that the king trusted Asaph with his own writings. He was **competent**, as the students he had were chosen for the job as well. He was **consistent** in his praise and worship of God. He wrote many recorded psalms.

In addition, during the reign of Hezekiah, Asaph's descendants were chosen to be trained as Seers for many kings after Asaph's time (2 Chron 35:15 "sons of Asaph").

Furthermore, 128 singing descendants of Asaph's returned from Babylon with Ezra (See Ezra 2:41) and performed during the dedication of the new temple (Ezra 3:10).

This is noteworthy because it was uncommon that a prophet or seer's children would follow in the ways of the LORD. (See 1 Sam. 8:1-3). Asaph's children and grandchildren followed in the ways of the LORD. That speaks volumes regarding Asaph's character and relationship with God.

Worship is a very important part of being a seer. It doesn't mean you have to have a wonderful voice or play an instrument. It does mean you need to be a worshiper. How does one worship?

O come, let us sing unto the Lord: let us make a
joyful noise to the rock of our salvation. (Psalm 95:1)KJV

Let us come before his presence with thanksgiving,
and make a joyful noise unto him with psalms.(Psalm 95:2)KJV

Make a joyful noise unto the Lord, all the earth:
make a loud noise, and rejoice, and sing praise. (Psalm 98:4)KJV

I love the Scriptures **make a joyful noise unto the** Lord. It's not about a beautiful voice or a well played instrument. It's about the attitude of your heart.

*How do you worship the **Lord**?

*Have you ever tried shouting or clapping your hands? If no, why not? Try looking up verses that have the word **Shout** or **Clap your hands** and see what God thinks about this type of noise.

*We have discussed Asaph's job. What do we know about his person? What kind of character did he have? Write down your observations.

I believe the third step to becoming a seer is working on your character.

Blessed are the pure in heart, for they shall see God (Matt. 5:8).

We all desire to see God. That's why we are taking this Bible study. But what is this about a pure heart? Let's look at some Scriptures for an explanation.

He who has clean hands and a pure heart, who has not lifted up his soul to an idol, nor sworn deceitfully. (Psalms 24:4).

In this Psalm we are asked who can ascend the hill of the LORD. Who may stand in His Holy place? The answer is one who had a pure heart.

[A Psalm of Asaph.] Truly God is good to Israel, to such as are pure in heart. (Psalm 73:1)

I love that this is one of Asaph's psalms. Again, a benefit of a pure heart is that God is good to you. The question is still- how do you get a pure heart?

Since you have purified your souls in obeying the truth through the Spirit in sincere love of the brethren, love one another fervently with a pure heart (1 Peter 1:22).

*Underline the phrase **since you have purified your souls**.

*Circle the phrase **in obeying the truth through the Spirit**. Remember in the first chapter it was discussed that everything is revealed through the Spirit? Earlier in this chapter the LORD says "Be holy, for I am holy." How is this possible?

Ever notice when two people spend a lot of time together they pick up each other's habits? They may start to have similar hand gestures or use similar phrases; or even begin to dress alike. They have spent so much time together they begin to emulate each other. It is the same with God. The more time you spend with God, the more you become like Him. God is faithful, gentle and kind. When you have spent time with Him, He will put a finger on an issue in your life. Because you have grown in love with God, you will want to please Him and change into His image. He will guide you through this process. It may or may not be painful; it is totally up to you. But during this process you gain a pure heart. You become "Holy as God is Holy".

"The statutes of the LORD are right, rejoicing the heart;
The commandment of the LORD is pure, enlightening the eyes"(Ps.19:8).

*How do you purify your heart? What are the results?

Lastly, I believe to become a seer it is important to learn how to be still.

Be still, and know that I am God; I will be exalted among the nations,
I will be exalted in the earth! (Psalm 46:10)

*Underline the first two words of this scripture. "Be still!"

Have you ever noticed that when you're all wound up and have lots of things going on, your insides tend to be in knots? It's impossible to hear anything or take in any new information. It takes real effort to be still. You must take a deep breath or maybe go for a walk. It takes being intentional to calm your insides. My friend, if you want to see in the Spirit, learning how to be still is crucial. But oh, the benefits: "and know!"

*Circle the third and fourth words in Psalms 46:10.

When you are still, you will know God. Jesus often went off to be alone with His Heavenly Father. He had to remove Himself from the demands of people and all the noise that comes with being around people. He had to quiet Himself. He had to find peace to receive His instructions from the Father. As you are learning to open your spiritual eyes, finding peace and quiet both around you and inside of you is an important step.

LORD, it's my desire to see You. I ask that You open my eyes to see You and know You. I praise you for all You have shown me. Prepare me to see more and more. Prepare me to understand what You want to reveal to me. Help me to quiet myself so I may hear and see more of You. In Jesus' name. AMEN

Let's recap:

1. One of the definitions for a Seer is one who sees in the spirit

2. How do I become a Seer?
    a. Ask (Elisha and his servant)
    b. Worship (Asaph)
    c. Character or Pure Heart(Matt 5:6)
    d. Be still and know

Journal Week Two

Day 1

*Play worship music and ask God to give you a vision. I'd like to suggest that you go to YouTube and listen to God of Wonders, Beyond Our Galaxy. Many renditions have amazing pictures of the universe.

*While listening, what images do you have?

*Do you see color?

*What do you feel? Goose bumps? Warmth?

*How did it expand your view of God?

*Write about it using this space.

Day 2

"Be still and know." Finding peace is very crucial. Think about the ways you try to de-stress after a busy day.

*Which methods work fast?

*Which ones take a little longer?

*Which method has a longer lasting effect? If you're preparing yourself to hear/see God, will any of these methods work?

*Use this space to write down your thoughts.

I find that if I do physical activity, my hearing is enhanced. But to see, I have to sit down and stop doing physically activity. I often listen to music, but I keep the volume very low. I often read a Scripture and meditate on the Scripture using my imagination. The Bible uses very descriptive language, so it's not too difficult if I am intentionally trying to see. The biggest challenge is quieting my mind. I will often write down on a piece of paper everything I'm thinking about- kids, projects, family, finances, etc. Then I pray and hand them over to God.

Sometimes I read a list of names of God, just to get my focus on God and who He is and what He is capable of.

I may do an exercise where I emphasize different parts of a Scripture. For example I will choose a Psalm because of the way it is written in phrases. I read it emphasizing the first phrase. I read it a second time, emphasizing the second phrase and so on. This will open my mind up to more possibilities to what God is saying in that Scripture.

*Let's try this exercise using Proverbs 4.

My son, give attention to my words;
Incline your ear to my sayings.
Do not let them depart from your eyes;
Keep them in the midst of your heart;
For they are life to those who find them,
And health to all their flesh.(Proverbs 4:20-22)

1.) Read the Proverbs passage all the way through.

2.) Read the Proverbs, emphasizing the first phrase. What was highlighted to you? Was there a picture you saw? Perhaps you saw a person looking at a Bible. Make a note of what you saw.

3.) Read the entire Proverbs, emphasizing the second phrase. What was highlighted to you? Perhaps an ear receiving notes. Did you see a picture? Make a note.

4.) Read the entire Proverbs, emphasizing the third phrase. Did you see a picture? Make a note.

5.) Read the entire Proverbs, emphasizing the fourth phrase. Make a note of what you saw.

6.) Read the entire Proverbs, emphasizing the fifth phrase. Make a note of what you saw or thought about.

7.) Read the entire Proverbs, emphasizing the sixth phrase. What did you discover?

8.) Take a moment to think about all that you noticed or saw in these three verses.

*Write down what you are feeling, what you are discovering and what questions you may have.

*Ask God those questions.

*Write about this experience.

*Now take time to ask God to give you a vision.

*Did it expand your meditations of this Scripture?

Day 3

Gatekeeper is one of the Hebrew words to describe a seer. Meditate on the word, **gatekeeper**. What do you think of? What do you envision a gatekeeper to look like? What are some responsibilities a **gatekeeper** might have? If you need to, look up in a dictionary what a gatekeeper may do. Do you see Jesus as a **gatekeeper**? Do you see yourself as a **gatekeeper**? Talk to God about your ideas and ask Him to expound what He wants to teach you about being a **gatekeeper** Go to a concordance and look up other verses that have to do with being a **gatekeeper** *What verses did you find? *What do they reveal about a **gatekeeper**? *Did God ever talk to the **gatekeeper** about his role, his behavior or his lack of responsibilities? *Write down your findings.

I want to take time to discuss the process of seeing in the Spirit. When I first began seeing in the Spirit, the picture was often in my peripheral vision. As I meditated on what I saw and talked to God about it, the picture would sometimes move to the center of my vision. At times I will still see a motion, not a picture, just motion-- in my peripheral vision and I still talk to God about it. I never pooh-pooh it. I want God to know He has my full attention. I take those motions or small pictures to be a way God is trying to get my attention. I want God to know I'm ready to see whatever He wants to show me, no matter how large or small.

Day 4

Another Hebraic meaning for **Seer** is **to establish, found, or fix**. Let's look at Scriptures with the word **establish**.

> "And as for Me, behold, I establish My covenant with you and with your descendants after you." (Gen. 9:9).

> But My covenant I will establish with Isaac, whom Sarah shall bear to you at this set time next year."(Gen. 17:21).

> And the dream was repeated to Pharaoh twice because the thing is established by God, and God will shortly bring it to pass." (Gen. 41:32).

*Who is the One who does the establishing?

If you see something in the Spirit, could God have something He wants to establish?

Notice how God shared with Noah, Abraham, and Pharaoh what He wanted to do. He wants to commune with us. Seeing in the Spirit is just one more way God wants to talk to us.

*Ask the LORD to give you a vision of something He wants to establish in your life. Write down what God gives you in this space.

*Ask Him questions about what you see.

*Look up Scriptures that make a reference to what you see.

*What are you emotionally feeling?

*Are you feeling something physically- tingling, goose bumps, warmth, or something else?

*Are you crying?

*Write about your experience in this space.

Day 5

Timely is another meaning for **Seer**. I love this verse.

"A person finds joy in giving an apt reply— and how good is a timely word!"(Pro. 15:23).

There have been so many times when God has given me a vision that I so desperately needed. It was timely and encouraging. For example once I was very concerned for one of my children and I just didn't know about their spiritual condition. I still remember vividly; I was driving our silver van through Freeland. I was by myself praying for my child. I looked at the passenger seat and I saw my child. She said "Mom, I can see. The colors are so bright. I can think, the noise in my brain is quiet. I feel so light". I started to cry and praise God. He had encouraged me that my child would be okay. He was doing something and I just had to believe and trust. This was such a timely vision. Now my prayers were not begging and lacking confidence, but rather declarations and thanksgiving.

*Bring to the Lord a situation you are concerned about. Quiet your heart and ask God to give you a timely vision.

*Write about what the Lord shows you.

*What comfort did you receive?

*Were there any instructions given to you? I knew the LORD was asking me not to give up, to keep praying and to keep trusting.

CHAPTER THREE
PURPOSE OF THE SEER GIFT

HAVE YOU EVER TRIED to give instructions to another person when they just don't understand? You try to explain it another way using different words. You still get the "deer in head lights" look. So you say "Let me show you!" That's how visions and the Seer Gift work. It's another way for God to communicate to you and further explain His plans. It's like words work in one part of your brain and pictures work to open up another part of your mind. Understanding is clearer and broader. It may lead to more questions, but the questions move the conversation along. A vision will often lead to furthering understanding.

Now it came to pass in the thirtieth year, in the fourth month, on the fifth day of the month, as I was among the captives by the River Chebar, that the heavens were opened and I saw visions of God. On the fifth day of the month, which was in the fifth year of King Jehoiachin's captivity, the word of the LORD came expressly to Ezekiel the priest, the son of Buzi, in the land of the Chaldeans by the River Chebar; and the hand of the LORD was upon him there.(Ezekiel 1:1-3)

*Circle the phrase **I saw visions of God**.

*Underline the phrase **the word of the LORD came expressly to Ezekiel**.

God used both visions and words to tell Ezekiel God's plan for his life. God's hand was upon Ezekiel as God was calling Ezekiel as a prophet to the nation of Israel. One of the purposes of the Seer Gift is to announce God's calling and purpose

And He said to me: "Son of man, I am sending you to the children of Israel, to a rebellious nation that has rebelled against Me; they and their fathers have transgressed against Me to this very day. For they are impudent and stubborn children. I am sending you to them, and you shall say to them, 'Thus says the LORD GOD.' As for them, whether they hear or whether they refuse—for they are a rebellious house—yet they will know that a prophet has been among them. (Ezekiel 2 3-5).

Another purpose to a Seer Gift is for God to give you understanding in whatever situation you're in. In Jeremiah's time there were many evil kings in Jerusalem. There were also many evil kings in the surrounding countries and there were always threats of war. God spoke to Jeremiah to help him understand what was going on and what the outcome would be.

And the word of the LORD came to me the second time, saying, "What do you see?"
And I said, "I see a boiling pot, and it is facing away from the north."
14 Then the LORD said to me:
"Out of the north calamity shall break forth
On all the inhabitants of the land.
15 For behold, I am calling
All the families of the kingdoms of the north," says the LORD;
"They shall come and each one set his throne
At the entrance of the gates of Jerusalem,
Against all its walls all around,
And against all the cities of Judah.
16 I will utter My judgments
Against them concerning all their wickedness,
Because they have forsaken Me,
Burned incense to other gods,
And worshiped the works of their own hands.
17 "Therefore prepare yourself and arise,
And speak to them all that I command you.
Do not be dismayed before their faces,
Lest I dismay you before them.
18 For behold, I have made you this day
A fortified city and an iron pillar,
And bronze walls against the whole land—
Against the kings of Judah,

Against its princes,
Against its priests,
And against the people of the land.
¹⁹ They will fight against you,
But they shall not prevail against you.
For I am with you," says the LORD, "to deliver you."(Jer. 1:13-19).

*What is the first question God asks of Jeremiah?

*What was Jeremiah's response?

Notice how God furthers the conversation by explaining what Jeremiah saw.

*Write out the last line of this section of Scripture.

God is so good. He encourages us even in the difficulties of life. This is another example of visions developing your relationship with God.

A further purpose of the Seer Gift is to give guidance and direction. Peter was waiting for dinner to be prepared and he went up to the rooftop to pray. This was very common and appeared unimportant; but God had other plans.

> *The next day, as they went on their journey and drew near the city, Peter went up on the housetop to pray, about the sixth hour. Then he became very hungry and wanted to eat; but while they made ready, he fell into a trance and saw heaven opened and an object like a great sheet bound at the four corners, descending to him and let down to the earth. In it were all kinds of four-footed animals of the earth, wild beasts, creeping things, and birds of the air. And a voice came to him, "Rise, Peter; kill and eat."*
>
> *But Peter said, "Not so, Lord! For I have never eaten anything common or unclean."*
>
> *And a voice spoke to him again the second time, "What God has cleansed you must not call common." This was done three times. And the object was taken up into heaven again. (Acts 10:9-16).*

God was giving Peter guidance and direction that he would need before he knew he needed it. God was expanding Peter's understanding of the Messiah and that salvation had come for all people- Jews and Gentiles alike.

*Underline the phrase **Saw heaven opened**.

Look at the phrase just before that; **fell into a trance**. Have you ever noticed there is a state of mind you are in just before you fall asleep? It's as if your body is winding down or finding peace so it can go to sleep. In my experience, when I am being still with God, meditating on a Scripture or listening to praise music, it is in that state of mind that I am prepared to receive from the LORD. I may receive words or pictures. But it is in that peaceful and quiet, trance-like state that I receive from God.

Also notice that God used pictures that Peter would understand. Peter was Jewish and knew Jewish law and which animals were unclean. God didn't need to take time to explain it. In fact, God left Peter pondering what it all meant. Moreover, something happened as Peter was thinking about it.

Now while Peter wondered within himself what this vision which he had seen meant, behold, the men who had been sent from Cornelius had made inquiry for Simon's house, and stood before the gate. And they called and asked whether Simon, whose surname was Peter, was lodging there.

While Peter thought about the vision, the Spirit said to him, "Behold, three men are seeking you. Arise therefore, go down and go with them, doubting nothing; for I have sent them." Then Peter went down to the men who had been sent to him from Cornelius, and said, "Yes, I am he whom you seek. For what reason have you come?"

And they said, "Cornelius the centurion, a just man, one who fears God and has a good reputation among all the nation of the Jews, was divinely instructed by a holy angel to summon you to his house, and to hear words from you." Then he invited them in and lodged them.

On the next day Peter went away with them, and some brethren from Joppa accompanied him. (Acts 10:17-23).

One of the Jewish laws was that a Gentile could not enter your house. Because of this vision, Peter allowed the men from Joppa to come in and even spend the night! Moreover, because of the vision, Peter knew what he was to do.

Additionally, a purpose for the Seer Gift is to encourage prayer and lead to declaration.

"You have heard;
See all this.
And will you not declare it?
I have made you hear new things from this time,
Even hidden things, and you did not know them.

They are created now and not from the beginning;
And before this day you have not heard them,
Lest you should say, 'Of course I knew them'. (Isaiah 46: 6&7).

At this point, God is using Isaiah to tell the people about God's frustration with them. God had told them things that would happen and yet they didn't turn back to God. God had revealed things to them, shown things that He, Himself wanted to do for them. All He asked was that they declare what God was going to do for them. God wants us to declare His promises even before they happen. He wants to build our relationship with Him (trust) and He wants to use us to build relationship with others (your God did what you said He would do)

Earlier in Chapter Two I discussed the different definitions of a seer. One of those definitions was **gatekeeper**. Another Hebrew word for **gatekeeper** is **watchman**. Isn't that interesting? What was a watchman's job? He was assigned to walk the walls of the city and watch. If anything approached the walls- a friend, a foe, or a storm--he was to sound an alarm. He would then wait for instructions from the King. Should the gate remain open or should it be closed? Should the armies be made ready, or should there be some other form of action?

*How does that relate to a Seer or one who sees in the Spirit? Write your thoughts.

How are God's plans known? How does He give instructions? God reveals Himself to you as you spend time in the Word of God by meditating on the Word, and by being quiet before God. By doing this you are allowing Him the opportunity to talk and reveal and show His plans to you. Your response to this revelation is to declare and speak out loud what God is going to do. In addition, praise and thank Him. He has it in His hands.

In the last chapter we discussed in the Journal section that another meaning for seer is **establish**. Could it be that God wants to use you to establish something? He is looking for a co-laborer. He is looking for someone to agree with Him and to declare it with faith. If He has shown something to you in the Spirit, before that something has come to be, God is revealing how much He trusts you and loves you.

Dear Heavenly Father, You have such good plans for me, but I don't know what they are. Please enlighten my spiritual eyes(Eph.1:15-19) to see You and know You and to have greater understanding. You are so faithful. Show me and teach me Your ways and what You would ask of me. Help me to see and declare Your wondrous ways. In Jesus' name, AMEN.

Let's recap:

The purpose of the Seer Gift is:

1. To develop your relationship with God
2. To know your calling and purpose(Ezekiel 1:1&2)
3. To give understanding in situations(Jeremiah)
4. To give guidance and direction(Peter on the roof top)
5. To encourages you to pray and declare (Isaiah 48:6&7)

Journal Week Three

Day 1

Developing relationship with God/Hagar

God opens a person's vision to develop a deeper relationship with them. In Gen 21, Hagar is the handmaiden of Sarah. She has been given to Abraham as a wife and she is pregnant. Hagar's ability to conceive has made Sarah jealous and she begins to mistreat Hagar. Sarah tells Abraham to send her away and he tells Sarah to do whatever she feels necessary.

Then Sarai said to Abram, "My wrong be upon you! I gave my maid into your embrace; and when she saw that she had conceived, I became despised in her eyes. The LORD judge between you and me."

So Abram said to Sarai, "Indeed your maid is in your hand; do to her as you please." And when Sarai dealt harshly with her, she fled from her presence.

Now the Angel of the LORD found her by a spring of water in the wilderness, by the spring on the way to Shur. 8 And He said, "Hagar, Sarai's maid, where have you come from, and where are you going?"

She said, "I am fleeing from the presence of my mistress Sarai."

The Angel of the LORD said to her, "Return to your mistress, and submit yourself under her hand." Then the Angel of the LORD said to her, "I will multiply your descendants exceedingly, so that they shall not be counted for multitude." And the Angel of the LORD said to her:

"Behold, you are with child,
And you shall bear a son.
You shall call his name Ishmael,
Because the LORD has heard your affliction.
He shall be a wild man;
His hand shall be against every man,
And every man's hand against him.
And he shall dwell in the presence of all his brethren."

Then she called the name of the LORD who spoke to her, You-Are-the-God-Who-Sees; for she said, "Have I also here seen Him who sees me?" Therefore the well was called Beer Lahai Roi; observe, it is between Kadesh and Bered.

So Hagar bore Abram a son; and Abram named his son, whom Hagar bore, Ishmael. Abram was eighty-six years old when Hagar bore Ishmael to Abram. (Gen 16:5-16).

Hagar had a visitation from an Angel. This strengthened her relationship with God. She saw God in a new light. She realized God did see her. Later in Genesis 19, God opened her eyes to see another well. Once again, God gave her vision to save her life, encourage her, and provide for her and her son. God's eyes are always open and His ears are always attentive to our needs (see 2 Chron. 7:15).

*Ask God to open your eyes to His provision, to His love for you. Let Him reveal Himself and His feelings to you in a new way.

*Ask Him to give you a vision to develop a deeper, closer relationship with Him.

*What did you see?

*What did you hear?

* Did you feel anything emotionally or physically?

*What new revelation of God did you receive?

*Write about your experience in this space.

Day 2

Discover what your calling and purpose is: Saul/Paul

Paul has been arrested and he is explaining to King Agrippa what has transpired in his life.

> "On one of these journeys I was going to Damascus with the authority and commission of the chief priests. About noon, King Agrippa, as I was on the road, I saw a light from heaven, brighter than the sun, blazing around me and my companions. We all fell to the ground, and I heard a voice saying to me in Aramaic, 'Saul, Saul, why do you persecute me? It is hard for you to kick against the goads.'
>
> "Then I asked, 'Who are you, LORD?'
>
> "'I am Jesus, whom you are persecuting,' the LORD replied. [16] 'Now get up and stand on your feet. I have appeared to you to appoint you as a servant and as a witness of what you have seen and will see of me. I will rescue you from your own people and from the Gentiles. I am sending you to them to open their eyes and turn them from darkness to light, and from the power of Satan to God, so that they may receive forgiveness of sins and a place among those who are sanctified by faith in me.'
>
> "So then, King Agrippa, I was not disobedient to the vision from heaven.
> (Acts 26:12-19 NIV).

*Underline verse 16. What is the purpose of Jesus appearing to Saul/Paul?

*Ask God to give you a vision of your purpose, your calling, and your talents. *What did you see?

*What did you hear?

*Did you feel anything emotionally or physically?

*What new revelation of your calling did you receive?

*Write about your experience.

Day 3

Gain understanding in a situation: Balaam

*Then God's anger was aroused because he went, and the Angel of the L*ORD* took His stand in the way as an adversary against him. And he was riding on his donkey, and his two servants were with him.*[23] *Now the donkey saw the Angel of the L*ORD* standing in the way with His drawn sword in His hand, and the donkey turned aside out of the way and went into the field. So Balaam struck the donkey to turn her back onto the road.*[24] *Then the Angel of the L*ORD* stood in a narrow path between the vineyards, with a wall on this side and a wall on that side.*[25] *And when the donkey saw the Angel of the L*ORD*, she pushed herself against the wall and crushed Balaam's foot against the wall; so he struck her again.*[26] *Then the Angel of the L*ORD* went further, and stood in a narrow place where there was no way to turn either to the right hand or to the left.*[27] *And when the donkey saw the Angel of the L*ORD*, she lay down under Balaam; so Balaam's anger was aroused and he struck the donkey with his staff.*

[28] *Then the L*ORD* opened the mouth of the donkey, and she said to Balaam, "What have I done to you, that you have struck me these three times?"*
[29] *And Balaam said to the donkey, "Because you have abused me. I wish there were a sword in my hand, for now I would kill you!"*

[30] *So the donkey said to Balaam, "Am I not your donkey on which you have ridden, ever since I became yours, to this day? Was I ever disposed to do this to you?"*

And he said, "No."

[31] *Then the L*ORD* opened Balaam's eyes, and he saw the Angel of the L*ORD* standing in the way with His drawn sword in His hand; and he bowed his head and fell flat on his face.*[32] *And the Angel of the L*ORD* said to him, "Why have you struck your donkey these three times? Behold, I have come out to stand against you, because your way is perverse before Me.* [33] *The donkey saw Me and turned aside from Me these three times. If she had not turned aside from Me, surely I would also have killed you by now, and let her live."*

[34] *And Balaam said to the Angel of the L*ORD*, "I have sinned, for I did not know You stood in the way against me. Now therefore, if it displeases You, I will turn back."*

[35] *Then the Angel of the L*ORD* said to Balaam, "Go with the men, but only the word that I speak to you, that you shall speak." So Balaam went with the princes of Balak . (Numbers 22:22-35).*

*What understanding did Balaam gain when the LORD opened up his eyes? (v.31)

*Ask God to give you a vision that gives you understanding into a particular situation.

*What did you see?

*What did you hear?

*Did you feel anything emotionally or physically?

*What new revelation to the situation did you receive?

*Write about your experience.

Day 4

Receive guidance and direction

> *[8] I will instruct you and teach you in the way you should go;*
> *I will guide you with My eye." (Ps. 32:8).*

*In what areas of your life do you feel lost or frustrated? Take an area and break it into smaller bites. Chose one of those bites to talk to God about and ask God to give you a vision that gives you guidance and direction.

*What did you see?

*What did you hear?

*Did you feel anything emotionally or physically?

*What new direction did you receive?

*Write about your experience.

Day 5

Pray and Declare

We have talked about the different meanings of **Seer** and we discovered that one of those meanings is **gatekeeper**. One of the things a **gatekeeper** does is to watch and guard and protect the gate, the entrance into the city.

Take heed, watch and pray; for you do not know when the time is. (Mark 13:33).

Continue in prayer, and watch in the same with thanksgiving. (Col. 4:2 KJV).

*What do you think a gatekeeper would do if he saw approaching danger? Take time to imagine it. *Write what you see.

If a gatekeeper is watching and he sees something, he will deal with it. He will shut the door. He will yell out at the intruders. That's what we are to do. We are to watch in the Spirit and ask God how He wants us to pray. When we receive instruction, we are to declare it loudly. A gatekeeper would not just whisper, "Shoo, wolf, shoo". **No-,** he would yell and shout and make noise to scare off the intruder. You are the gatekeeper of your home, your family, your friends, your church and even your place of employment. Keep watch and ask God what you are to declare. Follow this with thanksgiving. He has shown you the dangers. Ask Him what His plans are--His perfect will. Declare God's perfect will be done. Then rejoice in God's goodness. Thank God for what He wants to do and will do.

*Ask God what He wants you to watch or stand guard of; is it your children, your spouse or friend?

*Ask God to wake up your spiritual eyes to what He wants you to see.

I remember one time I was praying and asking God what was going on with one of my children. This child was just off, not being her normal self. I saw a dark dragon snake-like thing under her bed. I told it to leave in Jesus' name. I asked God to fill her room with His angels. I asked for peace and love and joy to fill her heart and mind. I declared that anything that was not of God must get out of my house. My house is the LORD's. I declared all the fruits of the Spirit to fill my home. I declared that my child was a child of God and she had the peace of God. By the next morning things were much better and I could see peace on her face.

*Who are you watching out for?

*Who are you guarding?

*Who are you a gatekeeper for?

*Ask God for a vision to help you understand what is happening.

*Ask God what to pray.

* Ask God what to declare.

*Write about what God reveals to you.

CHAPTER FOUR
SIMILARITIES BETWEEN PROPHECY AND SEER GIFT/ DIFFERENT WAYS TO SEE IN THE SPIRIT

LET'S COMPARE SEERS AND Prophets. They are mentioned together many times when a king's life is finished. Scriptures will refer to the exploits of a king and that they are written about by prophets and seers.

"Now the acts of King David, first and last, indeed they are written in the book of Samuel the seer, in the book of Nathan the prophet, and in the book of Gad the seer." (1Chron. 29:29).

"Now the rest of the acts of Solomon, first and last, are they not written in the book of Nathan the prophet, in the prophecy of Ahijah the Shilonite, and in the visions of Iddo the seer concerning Jeroboam the son of Nebat?" (2Chron. 9:29).

"The acts of Rehoboam, first and last, are they not written in the book of Shemaiah the prophet, and of Iddo the seer concerning genealogies? And there were wars between Rehoboam and Jeroboam all their days." (2 Chron. 12:15).

*Circle the words **Seer** and **Prophet**.

There is one verse that directly compares the two callings.

Formerly in Israel, when a man went to inquire of God, he spoke thus: "Come, let us go to the seer"; for he who is now called a prophet was formerly called a seer." (1 Sam. 9.9).

*Underline the phrase **for he who is now called a prophet was formerly called a seer.**

This verse leads us to believe that in the maturation process, a seer comes before a prophet. The difference between a prophet and a seer is that a prophet hears God's voice, whereas, a seer will see a vision with God expounding on its meaning. Let's look at another verse that talks about maturation. It is quoted in Joel and in Acts.

> *"And it shall come to pass in the last days, says God, That I will pour out of My Spirit on all flesh; Your sons and your daughters shall prophesy, Your young men shall see visions, Your old men shall dream dreams." (Acts 2:17.)*

Here maturation is discussed by young and old; the young will see visions and the old will dream dreams. What is important to understand is that age is not important to God. He will talk to children (example: Samuel was a child when he first heard the voice of the LORD.) and He will talk to the elderly. Maturation is more about our spending time with Him and our growing in our spiritual understanding.

Another example: When learning to read, youngsters are given picture books. As the youngsters grow in their ability to read, they are given books without pictures. When teaching a toddler to talk, one will show the toddler a picture of a dog and say **dog**. Talking to an older child, when they hear the word **dog**, they already have a picture in their head to match the word.

I believe that's why one may start as a Seer. God uses pictures and visions to grow communication with a person. It doesn't mean that a Prophet is of more importance, it is just communication is different. As we look at examples of both prophets and seers, we will uncover that both are in fellowship with God. God uses both the Prophet and Seer to communicate with God's people. Moreover, both are given insight to situations and are lead into times of intercession. Here is an example where both prophets and seers are used to talk to a group of people.

> *"Yet the LORD testified against Israel and against Judah, by all of His prophets, every seer, saying, "Turn from your evil ways, and keep My commandments and My statutes, according to all the law which I commanded your fathers, and which I sent to you by My servants the prophets.""(2 Kings 17:13).*

*Circle **all of His prophets** and **every seer**.

God uses both prophets and seers to talk to His people. Since we have been given the Holy Spirit, we too can receive messages and visions from the LORD.

Can the Seer Gift really be taught? Let's look at 2 Timothy.

> *Therefore I remind you to stir up the gift of God which is in you through the laying on of my hands. (2 Tim. 1:6).*

When someone lays hands on you, they pray for you, they impart to you. In this study, I have prayed for you. Through this study I am imparting knowledge to you. Now it is up to you to stir up the gift. You may ask, "How do I stir up a gift?" Here's what I do. I study the Word about that gift. I listen to others with that gift. I like to listen to teachings by Bob Jones on YouTube. I read books about the gift. Jim Goll and Patricia King both have books on the subject of being a **Seer**. In addition, I practice. I spend quiet time with the LORD often right before I go to bed. I pray over myself, asking for God's protection and wisdom over my mind. I ask Him to reveal or show me more of Himself. As I wrote this book I asked God to show me a picture of Himself. I saw a picture of Jesus carrying a lamb. I knew I was that lamb. I knew He was assuring me that He was carrying me through this process of writing and I could relax and rest on His shoulders. Then I try to think of a Scripture that will confirm the picture I've been given. In this case, the Scripture that talks about "the government is on His shoulders" came to mind. I felt encouraged that God has this Bible study all in His hands. I simply need to be still and I will know what to write and I just need to be obedient to write it.

When I receive a vision does it mean I am a **Seer** or a **Prophet**?

Remember we are NOT all prophets, but we are ALL are called to prophesy (see 1 Cor. 14:31). We are not all Seers, but we all can see in the Spirit. It is up to the LORD how far He will use this gift.

> *There are different kinds of gifts, but the same Spirit distributes them. There are different kinds of service, but the same LORD. There are different kinds of working, but in all of them and in everyone it is the same God at work. (1 Cor. 12:4-6 NIV).*

Ultimately, God is about the one. He left the 99 sheep to find the one straying sheep (see Luke15:4 and Matt 18:12). So He wants to use the seer gift primarily to encourage you and draw you closer to Him.

We are created in His image. We have five senses: touch smell, hearing, seeing and taste. I believe God wants to develop a communication language using ALL five senses.

A.W. Tozer wrote:

> *The Bible assumes as a self-evident fact that men can know God with at least the same degree of immediacy as they know any other person or thing that comes within the field of their experience. The same terms are used to express the knowledge of God as are used to express knowledge of physical things. "O taste and see that the LORD is Good." "All thy garments smell of myrrh, and aloes, and cassia out of the ivory palace." "My sheep hear my voice." "Blessed are the pure in heart, for they shall see God." These are but four of the*

countless such passages from the Word of God. And more important than any proof text is the fact that the whole import of the scriptures is toward this belief.

What can all this mean except that we have in our hearts organs by means of which we can know God as certainly as we know material things through our familiar five senses? We apprehend the physical world by exercising the faculties given us for the purpose, and we possess spiritual faculties by means of which we can know God and the spiritual world if we will obey the Spirit's urge and begin to use them.

That a saving work must first be done in the heart is taken for granted here. The spiritual faculties of the unregenerate man lie asleep in his nature, unused and for every purpose dead; that is the stroke which has fallen upon us by sin. They may be quickened to active life again by the operation of the Holy Spirit in regeneration; that is one of the immeasurable benefits which come to us through Christ's atoning work on the cross.

How awesome is this? It's no coincidence that you have this study in your hands. The Holy Spirit wants to wake up your sense of sight to communicate with Him! He loves you so much! So allow yourself to grow in this area. Do not fear. God is there to guide you. He is not an evil god who will trick you. He wants you to find Him!

"Call to Me, and I will answer you, and show you great and mighty things, which you do not know." (Jer. 33:3).

*Circle the word **show**.

*Underline the phrase **great and mighty things which you do not know.**

*What thoughts do you have after reading this? Write about them.

*Thank God for what He is revealing to you. Write your prayer here.

*Declare that you see in the Spirit and God gives you visions. If you don't know what to say out loud, ask God to help you. Have faith, He will help you. This is what He wants-- you to declare and speak His will out loud. *Write about your experience.

There are other similarities between Prophecy and Seeing in the Spirit. Both are meant to encourage, comfort, and edify (see 1 Cor. 14:3). Often times they both have symbols and will lead to you asking God questions. Remember, the purpose of both is to draw you closer to God. Asking and listening will bring you closer to God.

In addition, your response to a vision needs to be similar to your response when you hear a word from God. Your response should consist of the following:

1. Testing the spirits behind the vision.
2. Thanking God for the vision and wanting to reveal more of Himself to you.
3. Ponder, considering if there are any Scriptures that speak to the vision.
4. Ask God questions. What does this mean? What are you leading me to do?
5. Declare out loud what God has shown you.

Heavenly Father, You are maturing me. Thank You for opening my spiritual eyes to understanding. Give me wisdom on testing the spirits. Help me to take the time to ponder and ask questions. Give me revelation on what You want me to declare. In Jesus' name-AMEN

Let's recap:

There are many similarities between Prophesy and Seer gift

    a. Both encourage, comfort, edify
    b. Both draw you closer to God
    c. Both use symbols and often times you have to ask God questions to understand
    d. Your response to a vision is similar to your response to receiving a word from God

Not all people are called to be Prophet, but all can prophesy. Likewise, not all people are called to be Seers, but all can see in the Spirit.

Journal Week Four

Day 1

*Read John 10.

*Underline the word **shepherd.**

*Circle the traits or behaviors of a shepherd.

"Most assuredly, I say to you, he who does not enter the sheepfold by the door, but climbs up some other way, the same is a thief and a robber.[2] But he who enters by the door is the shepherd of the sheep.[3] To him the doorkeeper opens, and the sheep hear his voice; and he calls his own sheep by name and leads them out.[4] And when he brings out his own sheep, he goes before them; and the sheep follow him, for they know his voice.[5] Yet they will by no means follow a stranger, but will flee from him, for they do not know the voice of strangers."[6] Jesus used this illustration, but they did not understand the things which He spoke to them.

[7] *Then Jesus said to them again, "Most assuredly, I say to you, I am the door of the sheep.[8] All who ever came before Me are thieves and robbers, but the sheep did not hear them.[9] I am the door. If anyone enters by Me, he will be saved, and will go in and out and find pasture.[10] The thief does not come except to steal, and to kill, and to destroy. I have come that they may have life, and that they may have it more abundantly.* [11] *"I am the good shepherd. The good shepherd gives His life for the sheep.[12] But a hireling, he who is not the shepherd, one who does not own the sheep, sees the wolf coming and leaves the sheep and flees; and the wolf catches the sheep and scatters them.[13] The hireling flees because he is a hireling and does not care about the sheep.[14] I am the good shepherd; and I know My sheep, and am known by My own.[15] As the Father knows Me, even so I know the Father; and I lay down My life for the sheep.[16] And other sheep I have which are not of this fold; them also I must bring, and they will hear My voice; and there will be one flock and one shepherd.*

[17] *"Therefore My Father loves Me, because I lay down My life that I may take it again.[18] No one takes it from Me, but I lay it down of Myself. I have power to lay it down, and I have power to take it again. This command I have received from My Father."*

[19] *Therefore there was a division again among the Jews because of these sayings.[20] And many of them said, "He has a demon and is mad. Why do you listen to Him?"*

21 *Others said, "These are not the words of one who has a demon. Can a demon open the eyes of the blind?"*

22 *Now it was the Feast of Dedication in Jerusalem, and it was winter.* *23* *And Jesus walked in the temple, in Solomon's porch.* *24* *Then the Jews surrounded Him and said to Him, "How long do You keep us in doubt? If You are the Christ, tell us plainly."*

25 *Jesus answered them, "I told you, and you do not believe. The works that I do in My Father's name, they bear witness of Me.* *26* *But you do not believe, because you are not of My sheep, as I said to you.* *27* *My sheep hear My voice, and I know them, and they follow Me.* *28* *And I give them eternal life, and they shall never perish; neither shall anyone snatch them out of My hand.* *29* *My Father, who has given them to Me, is greater than all; and no one is able to snatch them out of My Father's hand.* *30* *I and My Father are one." (John 10:1-30).*

Now spend some time with the LORD.

*Ask Him to give you a picture in your mind of Jesus as the Good Shepherd. Imagine Jesus behaving as the Good Shepherd, you are the sheep.

*What is Jesus doing?

*What are you feeling physically?

*What are you feeling emotionally?

*Is this an easy process or is it difficult to stay in the picture?

*Write about this experience.

*Are there other images of Jesus in this passage?

*Spend some time with the L ORD meditating on these images.

*What do you see?

*Is Jesus there in the picture?

* Are you there?

*What are you feeling physically?

*What are you feeling emotionally?

*Does this encourage you?

*What could you declare about yourself or God after receiving this vision?

*Write about it.

*Spend some time with the Lord asking if there is more He wants to reveal to you. *What did God show you?

*Write about it.

Day 2

Read this section of Ephesians

Grace to you and peace from God our Father and the LORD Jesus Christ.

[3] Blessed be the God and Father of our LORD Jesus Christ, who has blessed us with every spiritual blessing in the heavenly places in Christ,[4] just as He chose us in Him before the foundation of the world, that we should be holy and without blame before Him in love,[5] having predestined us to adoption as sons by Jesus Christ to Himself, according to the good pleasure of His will,[6] to the praise of the glory of His grace, by which He made us accepted in the Beloved.

[7] In Him we have redemption through His blood, the forgiveness of sins, according to the riches of His grace[8] which He made to abound toward us in all wisdom and prudence,[9] having made known to us the mystery of His will, according to His good pleasure which He purposed in Himself,[10] that in the dispensation of the fullness of the times He might gather together in one all things in Christ, both which are in heaven and which are on earth—in Him.[11] In Him also we have obtained an inheritance, being predestined according to the purpose of Him who works all things according to the counsel of His will,[12] that we who first trusted in Christ should be to the praise of His glory. (Eph. 1:2-12).

*Circle the phrase **blessed us** in verse 3.

*Circle the phrase **He chose us** in verse 4.

*Circle the phrase **We should be holy** in verse 4.

*Circle the phrase **adoption as sons** in verse 5.

*Circle the phrase **made us accepted in the Beloved** in verse 6.

*Circle the phrase **we have redemption** in verse 7.

*Circle the phrase **the forgiveness of sin** in verse 7.

*Rewrite each of these phrases changing the **us** or **we** to your name.

*With these concepts in mind, ask God to reveal His feelings for you through a picture.

*What is the picture?

*Is God there?

*Is there a representative of God?

*Are you feeling encouraged or comforted?

*What other feelings are you having?

*Write about it.

*Ask God what He would have you declare about yourself. Write it down.

There is power in declaring or speaking out what the LORD has laid on your heart. God created the world by speaking. God wants you to learn to do the same. He wants to partner with you and establish His promises, plans, and purposes.

> *You will also declare a thing, And it will be established for you;*
> *So light will shine on your ways. (Job 22:28).*

Did you notice the word **establish** again. Interesting! The words **seer** and **declare** and **establish** are often mentioned in association with each other.

But how do you know what to decree? Spending time in the Word allow Gods to show you and speak to you about His plans.

> *"Now acquaint yourself with Him, and be at peace; Thereby good will come to you. Receive, please, instruction from His mouth, And lay up His words in your heart. (Job 22:21&22).*

*Circle the phrase **Now acquaint yourself with Him**.

*Circle the phrase **Be at peace**.

*Write about your thoughts.

*What is highlighted to you?

*What theme keeps coming up?

*How are you going to incorporate this into your life?

*Return to the section of Ephesians. Look at verse 9. What is His good pleasure?

*Is your confidence growing that God wants to reveal Himself to you? Write about it.

*Ask God what a partnership between you and He looks like.

*What did you see?

*How do you feel emotionally?

*What do you feel physically?

*How is your concept of God changing or growing?

*How are God's feelings towards you changing?

*Write about it.

Day 3

There have been times when I have seen evil things. One time I saw a dark blob that was going up my stairs. I told him to leave! He had no right to my house or my family. I prayed God's protection and I poured the blood of Jesus over our house and property. I didn't need to take a lot of time to test the spirits behind this vision. The character was dark and aggressive. That was all I needed to know. As it left I asked God what He was trying to reveal to me. Moreover, I spent time praising God for His goodness, faithfulness, and protection. I believe God will show me evil to warn me. I also believe Satan can try to intimidate me. However, I believe that what I give my attention to I will see more of. I want to see more of God. I want to glorify God and not give the enemy any credit or power in my life. I want to give God my full attention.

As you are learning to see in the spirit and to test the spirits; if it is not obvious as in the example above, be sure to take time to test the spirits. Ask if this vision is from God. Ask if the thing you see believes Jesus is the Son of God and sits at the right hand of God. By the time you start mentioning Jesus, if it is evil, it will flee.

*For today's journaling exercise I'd like you to pick one of your favorite worships songs to play. As you listen, get comfortable. Lie down or sit up. Pray, asking God to show Himself to you. (If you can't think of any songs, go to YouTube and find a rendition of The Revelation Song.)

*After you have listened to the song, write about what you saw.

*Was God somehow represented?

*Was Jesus somehow represented?

*What did you feel?

*What did you sense?

*What did you smell?

*What thoughts did the vision inspire?

*Is this vision suggesting some kind of action or change of thought?

*Write about it.

Day 4

As you go about your day, ask God to highlight a person you don't know. Ask God to highlight something about that person to you. It may be the color of their shirt, or something in their hand, it can be anything. Be open to what God has to show you. Then ask God how that highlighted object might lead you to pray.

Here's what happened to me when I did this exercise. I was in San Francisco and I was walking on a rail trail. God highlighted someone to me. God asked me to go and start a conversation. As I was talking to Him, the LORD highlighted the word **GIANTS** on his shirt. I asked the LORD what He was trying to tell me. He told me that this man had faced many giants and had had a lot of struggles in his life. God also told me that he was a giant in God's eyes. This man had great faith. I finished the conversation with the man, started walking away and asked God how He wanted me to pray for this man. God asked me to declare victory over the giants for this man and continued strength in his faith.

Your turn! Ask God to highlight a person to you. Don't worry-you don't have to talk to them, unless God tells you to. Ask God to highlight something about that person. Ask God how this highlighted object pertains to prayer. Pray!

*What did you see?

*How did it pertain to prayer?

*What did you feel?

*How did this affect your relationship with God?

*Write about it.

Day 5

*Ask God to give you a Scripture as a theme for the day.

*Write it down and carry it with you.

*Meditate on it.

*What pictures does it bring to your mind?

*What other scriptures correspond to it?

*Ask God for a vision to further explain what He wants to reveal to you through this Scripture.

*Write about it.

CHAPTER FIVE
DIFFERENT THINGS TO
SEE IN THE SPIRIT

There are many things you can see in the Spirit. I'd like to discuss a few of those.

Jesus

How awesome that Jesus would like to show Himself to us. In this example, there is a couple of men walking on the road to Emmaus. Jesus joins their walk. Jesus and the men talk and when it is close to sundown, the men ask Jesus to join them at their home. There He talks to them about the Scriptures and He gives them communion.

"Then their eyes were opened and they recognized him,
and he disappeared from their sight." (Luke 24:31).

This was pretty amazing because there was so much fear and doubt throughout the land. Jesus visiting them gave hope and understanding to continue in the faith that Jesus was the Messiah.

In my experience, I was in a conference during praise and worship, when I heard, "Come up here, I have great things I want to show you." (See Rev. 4:1) As I threw off any doubt and let my imagination take me upward, I saw Jesus. I ran to Him. I threw my arms around His waist like a little girl hugging her father. I felt warmth, comfort and assurance that everything was going to be okay.

Points I want you to take away from this experience:

1.) I knew Scripture and knew this was God. I was in praise and worship. My thoughts were toward God. I had to shake off any doubt that this could happen. There are many examples in the Bible of people seeing Jesus or going to the throne room. God doesn't show favoritism. If I'm willing to see in the Spirit, I will see in the Spirit. It's a free gift to all who ask. It is okay to imagine this yourself. Image what it would look like if Jesus was standing right in front of you. What would He be wearing? What would His facial expression be? Do you need a comforter? Do you need a warrior for your situation? Is that what Jesus looks like? *Write your thoughts and what you see?

2.) I also want to address how important it is to write down your visions. Visions can be simple: a door, a rose, a color. But a vision may also be long and very detailed. I've shared my experiences of both. Each vision was meaningful, timely, and left a mark on me. I encourage you to write your visions down and keep them. Sometimes when I need encouragement I'll read a past vision. I'm always able to recall it and it is as if I am back in the vision. I ask God to expand it. I ask Him what else He would like to show me. Habakkuk instructs us to write our visions down (see Hab.2:2-3). It will encourage us while we wait for the vision to come to pass.

Angels

In Acts 12 Peter is in jail for his faith. The church is praying for him. During the night, an angel appears to Peter and releases him from jail. Peter is confused and doesn't know if it is a vision or if it is actually happening. When he is outside of the jail and wakes up a bit more, he realizes the angel did free him. He went to the house where the church was praying for him. When he knocked at the gate, a girl comes to the gate. Hearing his voice, she becomes so excited she runs and tells the others. They don't believe it's really Peter, but think it's his guardian angel.

Points I want you to take away from this example:
1. Angels are not always easy to discern if they are from God.

   "Do not forget to entertain strangers, for by so doing some have unwittingly entertained angels."(Heb. 13:2).

   "And no wonder, for Satan himself masquerades as an angel of light"(2 Cor. 11:14NIV).

2. Angel's assignments consist of ministering to you, giving you a message, and protecting you.

   *"And He was there in the wilderness forty days, tempted by Satan, and was with the wild beasts; and the angels **ministered** to Him" (Mark 1:13).*

   *"For since the **message** spoken through angels was binding, and every violation and*

disobedience received its just punishment" (Heb.2:2 NIV).

*"For it is written: 'He shall give His angels **charge over you, To keep you,**'" (Luke 4:10).*

3. Angels are not to be worshipped.

"Let no one cheat you of your reward, taking delight in false humility and worship of angels, intruding into those things which he has not seen, vainly puffed up by his fleshly mind."(Col. 2:18).

One night, I was in bed and getting ready to fall asleep when I felt a presence on the bed. When I looked I saw a construction worker. I know that angels are God's messengers so I asked God what His message was for me. God told me that the angel was a builder and he was there to help me. Then I saw in the spirit the builder angel place big cut out blocks to form a road. They were about knee high when placed down. When I stepped on them, the block went down to street level, solidified.

When I asked God what this meant, He told me that He had builders laying out the foundation and what I was doing was solidifying what God wanted to accomplish. God encouraged me that we were working together.

I want you to notice I talked to God. I had a sense of peace, so I went to God to ask questions. There have been times when I'll ask the angel if it is from God. If it answers yes, I ask what message it has for me.

I also want you to realize that angels can come in different forms. I have had child angels visit me. I've heard testimonies of eagle angels visiting people. I have experienced seeing lights that are in shapes or form shapes. I always test the spirits and I always focus my mind on God, worshiping Him, or thinking of Scriptures that may explain what is happening. Accounts in the Bible talk about the lights around the throne. Also, I check my emotions. This is not my most important test, however. We are not to walk by our emotions. But if I sense a great amount of fear or confusion, I seek God as to if this is the enemy or if this is Him. At times I have experienced fear when I've had a vision because I serve an awesome God, and at times I am overwhelmed with His greatness. That's a healthy, godly fear.

Objects

There are times God will show you an object to speak to you. Jeremiah was asked by God "What do you see?" Jeremiah responded with "An almond branch." God continued to speak and explain what the almond branch meant.

> Moreover the word of the LORD came to me, saying,
> "Jeremiah, what do you see?"
>
> And I said, "I see a branch of an almond tree."
>
> 12 Then the LORD said to me, "You have seen well,
> for I am ready to perform My word."(Jer. 1: 11&12).

When you and I look at this we think **what**? God knows us so well; He will use pictures we will understand. The Hebrew word for **almond branch** sounds like the Hebrew word for **hasten**. God was revealing to Jeremiah that He was ready to take action.

Points I want you to take away from this example:

1.) God will speak to you in ways you will understand.

One time I was involved in a retreat and I was praying over the room where the teaching was taking place. I had a vision of grapes hanging from the ceiling. That was it. But I knew that anointing oil is made from grapes and when I see grapes I know it represents anointing. I began to declare that those who were teaching were anointed and that God was filling their mouths with His words. I declared that those listening had anointed ears to hear, eyes to see, hearts open to what God had for them that day.

Things highlighted to you

I have had experiences where God will highlight something to me. I shared previously about the man with the word **GIANTS** on his shirt.

I had a similar experience in a beauty parlor. I was at a mall getting my hair cut. I noticed that the beautician had chains on her boots and pants. I just couldn't stop looking at them. I asked the LORD what it meant. He told me that she was in bondage. She was tied in chains. I asked God if He wanted me to say something. He said **No**.

Later, as I was in my car, God told me to pray and declare for her. So I prayed for her salvation. I declared that she would be freed from the bondages that had her chained. I asked God to bring godly men and women into her life to guide her. I thanked God for trusting me.

Realize; I never saw her again. I don't know what happened. It's none of my business, it is God's. I know He loves her, that's why He sent me. He needed another spiritual warrior to pray and fight and declare for her life.

Points I want you to take away from this example:

1.) I have taught about character throughout this study. Having a godly character is crucial. Do I prove to be trust worthy? Am I obedient? Do I have a passion for God to be glorified or do I want attention?

2.) Are all visions to be shared? Absolutely not! God knew this young lady was not ready to hear she was in bondage. God is a tender God, full of loving kindness. He has to draw her close to Him before He can start working on her issues. It's about a relationship with Him, not a critical task master.

"And the vision of the evenings and mornings Which was told is true; Therefore seal up the vision, For it refers to many days in the future."(Dan. 8:26).

I have shared a lot of examples with you; however, God is a limitless God. I'm sure there are other things God can open your eyes to. As you spend time with Him and allow yourself to practice, God will reveal more to you. Remember you have to find a place of peace not just physically but mentally and emotionally as well. You must also deal with any doubt or fear you may have. God is a gentle God and He loves you so much. He won't give you more than you are ready for. However, realize He knows you better than you know yourself. He may give you more than *you think* you can handle. Just trust Him. You will get used to the new normal. You are the only one who limits your ability to see God.

Heavenly Father, You are amazing. You are so creative. You know me so well and know different ways to communicate with me. I choose not to fear or doubt. I chose to allow You to speak to me in these new ways. I declare that I do see in the Spirit and that I am Your co-laborer. I'm excited to see where this adventure takes me. I'm excited to see how many God stories we'll write together. You are amazing. Thank You for this gift of seeing in the Spirit. In Jesus' name, AMEN

Let's recap:

Different things you may possibly see in the Spirit
  1. Jesus
  2. Angels
  3. Objects
  4. Things which are highlighted to you
  5. Ask God, "What's a new way I can see something in the Spirit?"

Journal Week Five

Day 1

In the New Testament we are given the fruits of the Spirit.

> *But the fruit of the Spirit is love, joy, peace, longsuffering, kindness, goodness, faithfulness, gentleness, self-control. Against such there is no law." (Gal. 5:22-23).*

*Ask God to give you a vision of fruit.

*Ask Him what He is trying to show you.

*Write about what you saw and what God revealed to you.

Day 2

Throughout the Bible, God gives many names for Himself. In the Appendix of this study there is a list of names.

*Ask God which one He wants to use to reveal more of Himself to you.

*Ask God to give you a vision of the meaning of that name.

*Write about what you saw and what God spoke to you about.

Day 3

Armor of God

> *Finally, my brethren, be strong in the LORD and in the power of His might.[11] Put on the whole armor of God, that you may be able to stand against the wiles of the devil.[12] For we do not wrestle against flesh and blood, but against principalities, against powers, against the rulers of the darkness of this age, against spiritual hosts of wickedness in the heavenly places.[13] Therefore take up the whole armor of God, that you may be able to withstand in the evil day, and having done all, to stand.*
>
> *[14] Stand therefore, having girded your waist with truth, having put on the breastplate of righteousness,[15] and having shod your feet with the preparation of the gospel of peace;[16] above all, taking the shield of faith with which you will be able to quench all the fiery darts of the wicked one.[17] And take the helmet of salvation, and the sword of the Spirit, which is the word of God;[18] praying always with all prayer and supplication in the Spirit, being watchful to this end with all perseverance and supplication for all the saints—[19] and for me, that utterance may be given to me, that I may open my mouth boldly to make known the mystery of the gospel,[20] for which I am an ambassador in chains; that in it I may speak boldly, as I ought to speak. (Eph. 6:10-20).*

I had a vision that I was wearing the armor of a Samurai Warrior. It was many layers of padding. I knew every battle I'd been in had given me another level of padding. As I went over a bridge, I had a Samurai long sword. I extended my arm to give my sword to someone. As I brought my arm back, a longer, stronger sword was in my hand. Every time I gave away my sword, another stronger one was given to me.

I believe God was telling that I was well protected and every battle had served a purpose for me. I felt that God was encouraging me to keep giving the Word away (writing Bible studies) and that He would increase my sword of the Spirit (the Word of God in me).

*Ask God to give you a vision of the armor that you are wearing.

*What type is it?

*Are there any pieces missing?

*What color is it?

*Are there any kinks or damage?

*What is God telling you in this vision?

Day 4

God can use birds to speak to us. Look at the characteristics of the bird to help you understand. For example, God may show you an eagle. Eagles can fly very high and they can see their prey for miles away. Eagles often represent the prophetic.

God may show you an owl. An owl may represent wisdom. In addition, an owl can see things at night. It may be that God wants to reveal something that is hidden or in the dark.

God may show you a sparrow. Scripture tells us that God's eye is on the sparrow. It may be that God is telling you He is watching and aware of what is going on.

*Ask God to show you a bird. He may chose to highlight a bird at a birdfeeder or a bird flying over head. Don't minimize that. Realize God can use this method as well to show you something.

*What type of bird is it?

*What characteristics does it have? It's helpful to look up the type of bird in the Wikipedia or Google to find the characteristics.

*Are there Scriptures that mention that bird?

*What is God trying to reveal to you?

*Write about it.

Day 5

I'd like you to take some time to meditate on the following two Scriptures. Realize you are seated with God.

But God, who is rich in mercy, because of His great love with which He loved us,[5] even when we were dead in trespasses, made us alive together with Christ (by grace you have been saved),[6] and raised us up together, and made us sit together in the heavenly places in Christ Jesus,[7] that in the ages to come He might show the exceeding riches of His grace in His kindness toward us in Christ Jesus.[8] For by grace you have been saved through faith, and that not of yourselves; it is the gift of God,[9] not of works, lest anyone should boast.[10] For we are His workmanship, created in Christ Jesus for good works, which God prepared beforehand that we should walk in them. (Eph. 2:4-10).

If then you were raised with Christ, seek those things which are above, where Christ is, sitting at the right hand of God.[2] Set your mind on things above, not on things on the earth.[3] For you died, and your life is hidden with Christ in God. (Col. 3:1-3).

*Circle the phrase **made us sit together in heavenly places** in Eph. 2:6.

*Circle the phrase **sitting at the right hand of God** in Col. 3:1.

*Write about your thoughts.

*Is this a new concept to you?

*Have you ever thought about being seated at the right hand of God? That's how close God wants you to be.

*Think about and write about being in the presence of God.

It is perfectly okay for you to ask God to show you something or give you a vision. However, it is important that you have prepared yourself. Here are a few steps to help prepare you.

1. Check your heart. It is always important to ask God to search your heart. I John 1:9 talks about examining your heart and confessing your sins. Even the so-called little stuff counts: grumbling and complaining, little white lies, gossip or bad attitude. God is aware of it anyways, so why not be honest and deal with your sin? That way you are coming to God with a pure heart.
2. Be humble.
3. Ask the Holy Spirit if there is anything you need to confess or if you have any wrong thinking He wants to deal with. Wrong thinking or strongholds can block your ability to receive from the Holy Spirit.
4. Tell the LORD He has your attention. Ask Him, "What do you want to show me?"

In this exercise, I want us to take a look at the throne room and what Isaiah, Ezekiel and John saw. I want you to look for similarities and differences. Have you ever experienced when two people at the same scene describe what happened very differently? That's what happened with these three men. I don't doubt they saw what they described. However, when one has a vision, one doesn't always have the language to accurately describe it. Could this be why the three accounts have differences? I want you to look for characters in the scene. I want you to look for color or activity. I want you to notice any emotions that these men express.

Before you begin, let me pray for you.

*Father God, thank You for wanting to speak to us. Thank You for Your written Word that is our standard. L*ORD*, help us to understand Your Word. Open our minds to greater understanding. Quiet our fears and apprehensions. Open our eyes to see what You want to reveal to us. Thank You for Your kindness and gentleness. Thank You for meeting us right where we are at and desiring us to move closer to You. In Jesus' name, AMEN.*

ISAIAH'S ACCOUNT

In the year that King Uzziah died, I saw the LORD sitting on a throne, high and lifted up, and the train of His robe filled the temple.² Above it stood seraphim; each one had six wings: with two he covered his face, with two he covered his feet, and with two he flew.³ And one cried to another and said:

"Holy, holy, holy is the LORD of hosts;
The whole earth is full of His glory!"

⁴ And the posts of the door were shaken by the voice of him who cried out, and the house was filled with smoke.

⁵ So I said:

"Woe is me, for I am undone!
Because I am a man of unclean lips,
And I dwell in the midst of a people of unclean lips;
For my eyes have seen the King,
The LORD of hosts."

⁶ Then one of the seraphim flew to me, having in his hand a live coal which he had taken with the tongs from the altar.⁷ And he touched my mouth with it, and said:

"Behold, this has touched your lips;
Your iniquity is taken away,
And your sin purged."

⁸ Also I heard the voice of the LORD, saying:

"Whom shall I send,
And who will go for Us?"

Then I said, "Here am I! Send me."

⁹ And He said, "Go, and tell this people:

'Keep on hearing, but do not understand;
Keep on seeing, but do not perceive.'

10 *"Make the heart of this people dull,*
And their ears heavy,
And shut their eyes;
Lest they see with their eyes,
And hear with their ears,
And understand with their heart,
And return and be healed."

11 *Then I said, "Lord, how long?"*

And He answered:

"Until the cities are laid waste and without inhabitant,
The houses are without a man,
The land is utterly desolate,
12 *The Lord has removed men far away,*
And the forsaken places are many in the midst of the land.
13 *But yet a tenth will be in it,*
And will return and be for consuming,
As a terebinth tree or as an oak,
Whose stump remains when it is cut down.
So the holy seed shall be its stump."(Isaiah 6).

*Who are the characters in this account?

*What details stick out to you?

*What are Isaiah's emotions?

*What is his perception of God?

*Are there any instructions or directions given?

EZEKIEL'S ACCOUNT

Now it came to pass in the thirtieth year, in the fourth month, on the fifth day of the month, as I was among the captives by the River Chebar, that the heavens were opened and I saw visions of God.² On the fifth day of the month, which was in the fifth year of King Jehoiachin's captivity,³ the word of the LORD came expressly to Ezekiel the priest, the son of Buzi, in the land of the Chaldeans by the River Chebar; and the hand of the LORD was upon him there.

⁴ Then I looked, and behold, a whirlwind was coming out of the north, a great cloud with raging fire engulfing itself; and brightness was all around it and radiating out of its midst like the color of amber, out of the midst of the fire.⁵ Also from within it came the likeness of four living creatures. And this was their appearance: they had the likeness of a man.⁶ Each one had four faces, and each one had four wings.⁷ Their legs were straight, and the soles of their feet were like the soles of calves' feet. They sparkled like the color of burnished bronze.⁸ The hands of a man were under their wings on their four sides; and each of the four had faces and wings.⁹ Their wings touched one another. The creatures did not turn when they went, but each one went straight forward.

¹⁰ As for the likeness of their faces, each had the face of a man; each of the four had the face of a lion on the right side, each of the four had the face of an ox on the left side, and each of the four had the face of an eagle.¹¹ Thus were their faces. Their wings stretched upward; two wings of each one touched one another, and two covered their bodies.¹² And each one went straight forward; they went wherever the spirit wanted to go, and they did not turn when they went.

¹³ As for the likeness of the living creatures, their appearance was like burning coals of fire, like the appearance of torches going back and forth among the living creatures. The fire was bright, and out of the fire went lightning.¹⁴ And the living creatures ran back and forth, in appearance like a flash of lightning.

¹⁵ Now as I looked at the living creatures, behold, a wheel was on the earth beside each living creature with its four faces.¹⁶ The appearance of the wheels and their workings was like the color of beryl, and all four had the same likeness. The appearance of their workings was, as it were, a wheel in the middle of a wheel.¹⁷ When they moved, they went toward any one of four directions; they did not turn aside when they went.¹⁸ As for their rims, they were so high they were awesome; and their rims were full of eyes, all around the four of them.¹⁹ When the living creatures went, the wheels went beside them; and when the living creatures were lifted up from the earth, the wheels were lifted up.²⁰ Wherever the spirit wanted to go, they went, because there the spirit went; and the wheels were lifted together with them, for the spirit of the living creatures was in the wheels.²¹ When those went, these went; when those stood, these stood; and when those were lifted up from the earth, the wheels were lifted up together with them, for the spirit of the living creatures was in the wheels.

²² The likeness of the firmament above the heads of the living creatures was like the color of an awesome crystal, stretched out over their heads.²³ And under the firmament their wings spread out straight, one toward another. Each one had two which covered one side, and each one had two which covered the other side of the body.²⁴ When they went, I heard the noise of their wings, like the noise of many waters, like the voice of the Almighty, a tumult like the noise of an army; and when they stood still, they let down their wings.²⁵ A voice came from above the firmament that was over their heads; whenever they stood, they let down their wings.

²⁶ And above the firmament over their heads was the likeness of a throne, in appearance like a sapphire stone; on the likeness of the throne was a likeness with the appearance of a man high above it.²⁷ Also from the appearance of His waist and upward I saw, as it were, the color of amber with the appearance of fire all around within it; and from the appearance of His waist and downward I saw, as it were, the appearance of fire with brightness all around.²⁸ Like the appearance of a rainbow in a cloud on a rainy day, so was the appearance of the brightness all around it. This was the appearance of the likeness of the glory of the LORD.

So when I saw it, I fell on my face, and I heard a voice of One speaking

And He said to me, "Son of man, stand on your feet, and I will speak to you."² Then the Spirit entered me when He spoke to me, and set me on my feet; and I heard Him who spoke to me.³ And He said to me: "Son of man, I am sending you to the children of Israel, to a rebellious nation that has rebelled against Me; they and their fathers have transgressed against Me to this very day.⁴ For they are impudent and stubborn children. I am sending you to them, and you shall say to them, 'Thus says the LORD God.'⁵ As for them, whether they hear or whether they refuse—for they are a rebellious house—yet they will know that a prophet has been among them.

⁶ "And you, son of man, do not be afraid of them nor be afraid of their words, though briers and thorns are with you and you dwell among scorpions; do not be afraid of their words or dismayed by their looks, though they are a rebellious house.⁷ You shall speak My words to them, whether they hear or whether they refuse, for they are rebellious.⁸ But you, son of man, hear what I say to you. Do not be rebellious like that rebellious house;

open your mouth and eat what I give you."
⁹ Now when I looked, there was a hand stretched out to me; and behold, a scroll of a book was in it.¹⁰ Then He spread it before me; and there was writing on the inside and on the outside, and written on it were lamentations and mourning and woe. (Ezekiel 1&2).

*Who are the characters in this account?

*What details stick out to you?

*What are Ezekiel's emotions?

*What is his perception of God?

*Is Ezekiel given any directions or purpose for the vision?

JOHN THE REVELATOR'S ACCOUNT

After these things I looked, and behold, a door standing open in heaven. And the first voice which I heard was like a trumpet speaking with me, saying, "Come up here, and I will show you things which must take place after this."

2 Immediately I was in the Spirit; and behold, a throne set in heaven, and One sat on the throne.3 And He who sat there was like a jasper and a sardius stone in appearance; and there was a rainbow around the throne, in appearance like an emerald.4 Around the throne were twenty-four thrones, and on the thrones I saw twenty-four elders sitting, clothed in white robes; and they had crowns of gold on their heads.5 And from the throne proceeded lightnings, thunderings, and voices. Seven lamps of fire were burning before the throne, which are the seven Spirits of God.

6 Before the throne there was a sea of glass, like crystal. And in the midst of the throne, and around the throne, were four living creatures full of eyes in front and in back.7 The first living creature was like a lion, the second living creature like a calf, the third living creature had a face like a man, and the fourth living creature was like a flying eagle.8 The four living creatures, each having six wings, were full of eyes around and within. And they do not rest day or night, saying:

"Holy, holy, holy,
Lord God Almighty,
Who was and is and is to come!"

9 Whenever the living creatures give glory and honor and thanks to Him who sits on the throne, who lives forever and ever,10 the twenty-four elders fall down before Him who sits on the throne and worship Him who lives forever and ever, and cast their crowns before the throne, saying:

11 "You are worthy, O Lord,
To receive glory and honor and power;
For You created all things,
And by Your will they exist and were created."(Rev. 4.)

*Who are the characters in this account?

*What details sit out to you?

*What are John's emotions?

*What is his perception of God?

*Having read through these three accounts, what are the similarities?

*What characters were in all three accounts?

*What emotions did they have in common?

Remember the Ephesians and Colossians verses you read above? Ephesians tells you God has a great love for you. Colossians tells you to set your mind on things above. It is okay to meditate on the throne room.

*Ask God to give you a vision of the throne room. Don't be scared. Be open. God wants to reveal something of Himself to you. *Write your thoughts here.

I have seen the throne room from a great distance. I have seen the throne where God sits, but I could not see His face. Everything had a green tint and it seemed as if things were reeling around. I felt such awe, such peace, such wonder. I wasn't close enough to experience fear. Curiosity was my predominate feeling. Joy was also a strong emotion. I wanted to dance and twirl around. Then I noticed the elders. They were throwing their crowns before the LORD's throne. My thoughts went back to the holiness of God and I threw myself on the ground. I had nothing else to offer God. My heart was bursting with love and respect for my God. It was an amazing time with the LORD and I am honored and overwhelmed every time I think about it. What a blessing that God would chose any of us and that He wants to partner with us in anything. I pray that your vision of the throne room is as comforting, joyful and personal.

I can hear the nay-sayers and the fear rising. Let's think about this. When you go to a friend's house, do you barge in or do you knock on the door? You knock on the door, right? You may crack open the door and say, "Yoo-hoo, may I come in?" It's common courtesy to somehow ask if you may come into their dwelling place. It's no different with God, you can ask, "May I come in?" This is a process of humbling yourself and realizing you are talking to the Creator of the Universe. But also realize, His answer is always a resounding "Yes! Come!"

> *After these things I looked, and behold, a door standing open in heaven. And the first voice which I heard was like a trumpet speaking with me, saying, "**Come** up here, and I will show you things which must take place after this."(Rev. 4:1).*

> *Let us therefore **come** boldly to the throne of grace, that we may obtain mercy and find grace to help in time of need. (Heb. 4:16.)*

Realize, just as this Bible study started with Tozer saying God is close and it has everything to do with your receptivity, God wants to show you things. He wants to talk to you. This last exercise may be a stretch, but don't shy away from it. Keep trying. Keep allowing your gift to grow. Keep testing what you see. You will find that it will match up with the Word of God. God loves you deeper than you will ever know. How fun to discover there is more!

Go back and again ask God to give you a vision of the throne room. It may be a very small corner. God is gentle. He will give you what you have faith for.

*Write what God shows you.

CHAPTER SIX
I'VE HAD A VISION! NOW WHAT!?

YOU HAVE SOUGHT GOD and you have found Him (see Jer. 33:3). God has given you a vision. Now what do you do?

1. Write it down (Habakkuk 2:2).
2. Test the Spirit (see 1 John 4:1-3).
3. Ask God what He wants you to do with it. Are you to share it? Are you to pray about it? Is it something God wants you to declare?
4. Thank God for it. After I write down my vision, I write down the answer to #3 and a thank you prayer to God.
5. TRUST, WAIT and REST.

*Look up Proverbs 3:5&6. Write it down. How does it pertain to a vision?

*Look up Isaiah 40:31. Write it down. How does this pertain to a vision?

God has given you a vision. He wants to talk to you. Have peace. Trust God and His goodness towards you. Some things you see may not make sense right away. Relax. It's okay. When you were in school did you understand every math formula or chemistry concept right away? No! Some things take time. God is patient and He is loving. As long as you are seeking Him and are not in a rush or a panic, the understanding will come forth. Also, there are times when God is speaking in puzzles or parables and wants to continue the conversation. You will understand it at the right time. This is why it's important to write your vision down. Sometimes they have to maturate in your spirit. Keep trusting and waiting and believing God has something good in store for you! REST!

Closing

Thank you so much for joining me on this adventure. I know God is faithful to open your spiritual eyes as you seek Him. He is a trustworthy God. He is a creative God. It is always exciting to spend time in God's presence. I am forever changed every time I make the effort. I pray that this study has encouraged you to seek God and not fear. I pray my examples have opened your eyes to possibilities, but not to comparison. Remember, God uses a personal form of communication. What will your visions be like? Don't worry if it is just a mist or a hue. Don't worry if you only see in your peripheral vision. Don't worry if you don't understand what it means. Ask God questions. The more you know God and spend time with Him, the more you'll be able to open your spiritual eyes and give your full attention to God. Just think about the wonders He will show you!

APPENDIX

List of Meanings of Colors

Here is a list of the meaning of colors. This may help you understand what God is saying in your vision if colors are highlighted. The meanings of colors are explained in the Bible study *How to Hear God's Voice: Intro to Dream Interpretation.*

White (+) Spirit of the LORD, holy power; (-) religious spirit

Red (+) wisdom, anointing, power; (-) anger, war

Green (+) conscience, growth, prosperity; (-) envy, jealousy, pride

Blue (+) communion, revelation; (-) depression, sorrow, anxiety

Yellow (+) mind, hope, gift of God; (-) fear, coward, intellectual pride

Orange (+) perseverance; (-) stubbornness, strong-minded

Purple (+) authority, royalty; (-) false authority, licentiousness

List of Names of God

El Elyon: The God Most High

El Olam: The Eternal God

El Roi: The God Who Sees Me

El Shaddai: The All Sufficient One, the God of the Mountains, God Almighty
Immanuel: God with Us

Jehovah: "I Am"; The One Who is, The Self-Existent One

Jehovah-Jirah: The LORD Will Provide

Jehovah-Mekaddishkem the LORD Who Sanctifies, Justice

Jehovah-Nissi: The LORD is My Banner

Jehovah-Rapha: The LORD Heals

Jehovah-Rohi: The LORD is My Shephard

Jehovah-Sabaoth: The LORD Of Hosts, The LORD Of Armies

Jehovah-Shalom: The LORD is Peace

Jehovah-Shammah: The LORD is There, The LORD My Companion

Jehovah-Tsidkenu: The LORD is Our Righteousness

Suggested Reading List

Goll, James, The Seer Expanded Edition: The Prophetic Power of Visions, Dreams, and Open Heavens

Footnotes:

1 A.W. Tozer, Compiled by James L. Snyder, *The Essential Tozer Collection (New Your; Bethany House, 2013), 64-67.*

www.ingramcontent.com/pod-product-compliance
Lightning Source LLC
Chambersburg PA
CBHW062111090426
42741CB00016B/3393